*This book is dedicated to Adnan Sarhan,
who showed me that real success is
the treasure hidden within each of us
and the key to opening it
is the moment in our hand.*

Overcoming the 7 Devils That Ruin Success

James Dillehay

WARM SNOW PUBLISHERS
TORREON, NEW MEXICO

Special thanks to Adnan Sarban for his generous support and encouragement, Michelle Peticolas for editing with a firm, but loving hand, Janet Norquist for her devilish designs, Allan Verdegraal for his helpful critique and John Paul Deoliveira for his thorough proofreading.

Published by:
Warm Snow Publishers
P.O. Box 75
Torreon, NM 87061

Cover design by Janet Norquist
Edited by Michelle Peticolas, Ph.D.

ISBN: 0-9629923-1-3
Library of Congress Cat. Card No.: 93-094313

Printed and bound in the United States of America

 Printed on recycled, acid-free papers ∞

Contents

The Heart of the Matter

When I was seventeen, I knew that I wanted to study the self, to learn what a human being is ultimately capable of experiencing. I imagined that psychology would be the reasonable choice of study. However, I found college courses focusing mostly on aberrant behavior, not on questions like *"Who am I?"* I somehow had formed the presumption that the learning I sought came from direct experience, not from memorizing statistics.

My desire seemed out of sync with what my parents and teachers said were important. Compared to society's view of success, my notions were impractical, if not absurd. I began to disbelieve in what I wanted, because everyone that mattered agreed that happiness and success were tied to getting a college degree, rising in business, and earning a high salary.

Yet, these prospects failed to inspire me. I couldn't see working years toward a degree in a field for which I felt no connection. Resigned, I dropped out of college and took a job in a grocery store. It was hard to avoid the feeling that I had not measured up, that I had failed.

At least, the job paid the bills. It also motivated me to look for alternate ways to achievement including self-development. I became interested in books on Eastern thought and spirituality. However, it was in the writings of Western researchers, like Robert Ornstein, M.D.'s *The Psychology of Consciousness,* where I learned of an intriguing people called Sufis whose practices develop higher intelligence and awareness. Their traditions do not seem bound to any particular culture or race. It appears that the Sufi seeks development within the existing cultural framework in which he or she finds themselves in a way not meant to threaten that framework, but transform it, allowing the person to evolve inwardly and outwardly.

According to *The Sufis,* by Idries Shah, Science and the Arts owe more to Sufi influence than is popularly known. Algebra, for example, originated with and was named after a Sufi named Al Jabir. More well known Westerners whose lives were positively inspired by Sufis include Chaucer, Roger Bacon, William Shakespeare, and Sir Richard Burton the explorer.

As I read about Sufis, I saw examples of people who had made contributions of achievement to the world, as well as attained practical means for bringing heightened states of awareness and perception. I couldn't have guessed, before I eventually encountered this specialized training, how much it would dramatically redefine my own experience of accomplishment. Nor, could I have imagined how forces within my own personality were sabotaging me all along.

Sufi texts sometimes refer to the primitive stage of development in the personality as the negative or animal self. Freud was also aware of this animalistic nature and identified it as a principal driving force of the id. He theorized that it is fueled by a "death wish" which leads organic life back to an inanimate condition.

This negative self gives rise to self-defeating tendencies which I have likened to devils, because their ruinous effects give the appearance of willful, malevolent intent. When we are under their influence, there is the feeling of being a victim of a sinister plot. In this case though, the scheme originates inside us, not from somewhere outside.

The devils of the negative self rob us of both energy and will power, allowing us to become victimized by others eager and ready to take advantage. If we let them, employers will use guilt to squeeze more and more sacrifices from us, like working late and on the weekends. Advertisers will use our habits of response to sell us products we do not need. These others persuade us, though, only when we are slaves to the devils in ourselves. If, however, a person confronts and conquers these devils, an inner force is released and comes back to him or her.

We are most susceptible to these devils when we aren't doing what we really want with our lives. Here, 'doing what we want' goes deeper than gratifying idle whims. Inside each of us, there is an important faculty called the intelligence of the heart. This intelligence is the source of intuitive perception, or knowing without thinking, that guides us to discover our true desires. When intelligence of the heart is active, the natural source of creativity is awakened. The person experiences penetrating insights and sees what the right thing to do is in any situation.

In his book of Sufi teaching stories, *The Enchanted Oasis of the Ringed Dove,* Adnan Sarhan says:

". . . the intelligence of the heart bypasses the intellect in the head which works on assumptions and requires a lot of thinking and confusion and makes a person tired and weak. But, the heart intelligence is not only direct and to the point, it also gives you energy, vitality and strength."

An aim of *Overcoming the Seven Devils that Ruin Success* is to create a recognition of the natural source of intelligence within. This wisdom is available at any time, though we may not see it because of one or more of the seven devils. Within the powers of the intelligence of the heart lies the ability to guide us to serenity, contentment, and the source of life. From that inner source, we will become healthier, happier, and more successful in practical ways.

Few people are clear from the start about what they really want in life, becoming more certain only after experience. We can learn what holds the most fulfillment for us through trial and error. The way to do that is to measure an activity by how you feel afterward. If what you do makes you feel inspired, expanded, energized, playful, satisfied, or content, then this means you are doing the right thing for yourself.

If an activity makes you feel tense, nervous, contracted, angry, obsessed, tired, or frustrated, you are doing the wrong thing. When you feel any of these, they are signs of the seven devils at work.

In this book, when I say achieving success, I don't mean making a million dollars or becoming famous, though that could easily come after you find what you really want. The experience and pleasure of success comes in doing what is vitalizing and energizing for you. The first step toward learning what fulfills your heart's desire is to recognize what does not, as when the devil of false success casts its spell of illusion.

The First Devil:
False Success

False success means abandoning what is important in your heart for the lure of money and security. When we primarily strive for more and more money or possessions, we will never get enough to satisfy. There will always be a better job, a newer car, or a bigger house. Whatever we gain in material success will never be enough, because these desires for "more" arise from conditioned social drives, not from real needs.

The media creates unrealistic role models through glorifying the millions of dollars earned by rock idols, football quarterbacks, and television anchor-persons. Since childhood, we have been exposed to endless social signals that tell us winning equals success and losing means failure. Our real loss is that by comparing ourselves to the artificial media version of success, we overlook the reliable source of happiness at hand, our own wisdom of the heart. There's a danger, too, that if one ignores the natural source of intelligence within for too long, it becomes dormant and forgotten.

One may become so caught up in winning that awareness of reality is subverted to the driving forces of ambition and greed. Obsessed only with success, this person is in danger of trading his warmth and humanity for the shadow of false success.

For several years while in my early twenties, I managed convenience stores. I finally grew tired of being robbed at gunpoint and blamed for endless shortages by a supervisor who was later fired for embezzling. At my mother's urging, I went to work at my father's company, a chain of career clothing stores in Houston.

He began the business from home while working a full time job and supporting a family of six. After several years of hard work, he and my mother managed to build it into four stores.

Their accomplishment was a vision of success. Shortly after I joined, my father incorporated the business and named me vice-president. Together, we planned to open more stores, buy land for shopping centers, and expand into other kinds of businesses.

I saw my new position as a promise of financial security. My parents expected me to continue the business they had so painstakingly built from nothing. However, I never asked myself if this was what I really wanted to do. It seemed that if I were going to surrender to the world's model of success, this was the best role I would ever get.

Around this same time, I met the man who became my teacher, Adnan Sarhan, while he was traveling and teaching in America. Originally from Baghdad, he was born with a heritage of Sufi experiential knowledge and grew up under the influence of spiritual teachers in a cultural tradition where everyday life and spiritual development had been interwoven for thousands of years. His unique talent seems to be in his abilities to make Sufi traditions that originated in the Middle East, both accessible and palatable for Westerners.

Adnan is known for the *"Shattari,"* or "rapid method," of developing higher intelligence and awareness. He uses many Sufi techniques including physical exercise, breath, chanting, whirling, meditation, and dance.

I found his teaching methods penetrated on many levels. My mind became more settled and my thoughts clearer. Also, my vision improved while my body developed increased strength, flexibility, and a sense of readiness. I often came away from these workshops with the feeling that I had just awakened to a brighter, more hopeful reality. This feeling lasted long after the workshops and began to grow.

The more of the training I did, the more I wanted to explore it further. I decided to attend a summer retreat with Adnan in the mountains of North Carolina. It was here that he had a brief talk with me which dramatically changed the course of my life.

One day after a lengthy exercise session, everyone in the group went outdoors to rest and talk. I was sitting on a low stone wall and Adnan came over to sit beside me. After a few casual comments, he told me that I should quit my job, that it would only hold me back in the work I would be doing later. Suddenly, reality collapsed and expanded around that single statement. The bridge of safety and assurance I had built upon my future business plans just disintegrated, spilling me into a wild current of unknown waters. Yet, I could not bring myself to disagree with him, his sense of calm command overrode the impulse to argue my position. Seemingly indifferent, he got up and walked away without waiting for me to reply.

I had given him few details about my life. Yet, he spoke with the calm authority of knowing exactly what I had been doing and what I should do next. It was also as if he was telling me something about myself that I already knew but had been unable to admit.

I felt, too, that I wasn't ready to accept it. He was telling me to give up the future security I was working toward, and in effect, turn away from my family. Despite my desire to learn more from this exceptional teacher, I could not fathom his purpose in interfering with my personal affairs.

Granted, I wasn't particularly happy, but how could this man from a culture on the other side of the globe begin to comprehend my situation? At the age of twenty-four, the prospect of one day running a successful corporation outweighed almost any other consideration.

Few people I had met really enjoyed what they did for a living. Even fewer seemed to live out their dreams. It seemed I had forgotten my own dream in the lure of material wealth and social status.

Adnan's advice left me deeply troubled, but shortly after our conversation took place, I returned to Texas. I told myself that I couldn't afford to think about what he had said; ambition called, not to mention responsibility and obligation. On arriving home, everything was just as I had left it, my desk was stacked with papers to sort and record and business was going on as usual.

There was, however, a singular, extraordinary difference; I had changed. I found myself accomplishing more tasks with less efforts. In situations where I would have been hesitant, I acted decisively. Instead of avoiding people, I communicated with them. My sales rocketed and I felt dynamic.

Several months passed bringing increased improvements in my skills and insights. Despite the obvious (to me) cause for these changes, I spoke little to my parents about the Sufi work. I expected them to put it down as my imagination or wishful thinking. During this time, I sometimes reflected inwardly on Adnan's advice to quit, but my doubts about what to do only left me more confused.

As I continued to become more successful at the business, I noticed the stirring of impulses that I can only call Machiavellian. I began to value people in terms of how much they owned or how much power they wielded. I also fantasized how much I would one day control. It was as if a shadow self was gradually replacing the warmth toward others I remembered once feeling. There was also a sense that I was losing my youth, even though I was only twenty-four years old.

As summer neared again, however, my previous experiences with Adnan's Sufi training drew me to return to work with him. I planned to keep my job, but somehow arrange to take time off to go to the next workshop. Unfortunately, the choice wasn't going to be that simple. A few months before the next summer workshop was to begin, my father told me that he was arranging a loan which would enable me to buy the corporation from him.

From that moment, every day at work became torturous. Conflicting desires — one for wealth and status, the other to study with Adnan — waged war in my poor, beleaguered brain. My new strengths and confidences reminded me of how much I already owed to the Sufi work. Yet, it seemed foolish to walk away from the easy opportunity for success about to be handed over. Reason said to stay, but a deep, still voice within said to go.

In the midst of my turmoil, I one day found myself sitting alone in my office with nothing to do. As I stared blankly at the wall, I fell into a dream like state where I saw a road stretching out before me. At some point, the road forked in two directions. Following one path to the end, I saw myself as an old man, very rich, with tears on my face. I was weeping because I had passed up the opportunity to do what my spirit really yearned for.

Suddenly, I was back at the fork looking down the other path. I couldn't see anything there except a misty cloud that obscured the road and what lay ahead. I knew without a doubt this was the path of the Sufi. I could see, too, that this path offered no promises. If I went this way, I would make my own destiny.

After months of agony, I knew I had finally come to a decision. Taking the irrevocable step, I left my father's business forever. At the time, I couldn't find the courage to tell either of my parents to their faces. I feared I would never hold to my resolve under their "reasonable" arguments. If I thought about it too much, what I was doing did seem crazy. I told them I was simply going on a vacation. Once safely away, I wrote them a letter explaining that I would not be back. My heart's desire had won out, but at what cost? I had turned my back on the parents who had raised me and cast away a fantastic opportunity that I was sure would never come again.

When they read my letter, of course, both my parents were hurt and disappointed. My father put the business up for sale anyway and soon found another buyer. I wanted distance from the whole matter, so I left Texas to look for whatever work I could find in Colorado.

Shortly afterward, the world oil glut instigated an economic crisis in the Houston area. Because Texas was a center for the oil industry, both major and independent oil companies reeled from plunging prices. Thousands lost their jobs. Real estate developers who had speculated highly in Houston area properties went bankrupt. Several huge banking groups that financed them also collapsed. Some of my father's competitors folded, including the group who had bought his company.

If I had stayed with the business, I would probably have lost everything. What could an untried youth have done against such unexpected odds when huge, successfully run conglomerates were falling all around? Fortunately, my father got his money out before I had a chance to lose it for him. For myself, I had narrowly escaped my inner devil of false success who would surely have stolen my soul and the promised wealth, too.

Afterward, I was on my own without the security of a future I had once imagined for myself. I was free to plot my own course though, and in the following months, I went from one kind of work to another, trying different things. If I didn't like a particular job, I simply left. No misery seemed worth a few dollars an hour. In this process of exploration, I met new challenges, learned different skills, and gained an attitude of flexibility that had never been possible for me before.

I felt a growing desire to merge what I wanted to do with making a living in the world. I also wanted to create my own accomplishments and feel connected to my work. In light of this, I eventually came to suspect any impulse that suggested *"Make money first, then you'll be happy."* I also found myself wondering if Adnan had foreseen all of these events and presented me the opportunity to escape my devil of false success.

Any job, regardless of how good it looks on the surface, is inherently insecure. Mysterious, unseen economic forces or natural disasters can quickly undermine the best of plans. Real security lies in knowing yourself. Opportunities for starting your own business are plentiful if you are willing to do some homework. Of course, if you have a job that pays good money and you like it, there's no reason to make a change. You might be ready, however, when everything on the surface seems to be going well, but inside a small voice asks, *"Is this all there is?"* If you are unsure of your own needs, consider asking yourself the following questions. Note: you'll get more objective answers if you put some distance between you and the situation, like a vacation, for instance:

- Is there something else I always wanted to do, but never felt I could afford the time for?
- If I lost my job, would I see it as a tragedy or an opportunity?
- Am I working for money or for love of what I am doing?
- Does work depress me, am I often tense and irritable?
- Am I drinking a lot of coffee to get through the day, compulsively eating, smoking more when under tension, or needing to get drunk after work or on the weekends?
- Do I expect to be any happier later in my life than I am now? Why?
- Would I stay with my current job if I didn't have to worry about money?
- Have I set aside my dreams for someone's good opinion of me?

- Am I waiting for some future time when life will suddenly become happier?

For many, the frustrations of living out the expectations of employers, family, and spouses may finally make them ask, *"When do I get to do what I want?"* It's one thing to recognize your own needs, it may be more difficult to find the strength to seek their fulfillment. Perhaps we resist because it may mean making changes and moving away from past ties. Will freedom from false success, in of itself, guarantee more satisfying accomplishments? We cannot know without trying. Standing guard before the entrance to new opportunities, we will meet the devil of fear. To enter a happier future, we may have to let go of who we were in the past. We can either let go willingly, or inevitably, reality will force us to move forward anyway.

The Second Devil:
Fear of Change

Fear is an instinctual reaction to danger. It is a primal, visceral response which when stimulated, usually produces intense chemical changes in the body. Those changes prepare us to fight or flee a threat. Fear can also be so intense at times we are terrified to the point of paralysis.

The fearful reaction originates with an actual event where there was a real or perceived danger. In many cases, however, fear can become restimulated as a habitual response long after the original danger has passed. When this happens, we respond to imagined threat, not the reality. Negative associations enforce thinking patterns and behavior that later return to block us from seeing or acting freely in a given situation like the one below. Fearful reactions thus become habitual or phobic.

Once, I was staying for a few weeks at a large farm with a diverse group of people who had all come for a seminar. At the end of the sessions, I enjoyed walking across the pastures at night alone, looking at the stars. One night while I was out for my stroll, I heard a woman crying for help.

Her voice sounded desperate, so I ran in the direction of her shouts as fast as I could even though it was dark and hard to see. Her screaming became more hysterical as I got closer, but I couldn't tell where she was, because all around me, large dark shapes blocked my way. Suddenly, I realized that I had run into a herd of cows and that the woman was in the center of them.

I called to her, *"What's wrong? Are you hurt?"*

"I can't move, I'm afraid of the cows," she cried.

I said, *"Just walk to me, they won't hurt you."*

"Help me," she wept, *"I'm too afraid."*

It was obvious she was unable to get past her terror, so I walked through the cows to where she was. Giving her my arm to hold onto, I guided her out of the herd to a clear place.

Though there was no actual danger, she was not ready to face her phobia. This woman's experience may seem extreme, but unreasonable fear can become an obstacle to getting free of our own mental herd of cows.

Fear of changing our lives can be overcome only when we want to change even more than we want to stay stuck. The process starts with thought patterns. If we say *"I can't"* to anything in life, that becomes the truth. If we're afraid to ask for a raise, that may be just a habit of fear. Unless we are willing to act on our real needs, those fears will always leave us self-defeated.

Even if you believe without a doubt that you're incapable of accomplishing something, don't play the tape *"I can't."* In your mind and in your speech, replace this denial with the positive affirmation *"I can"* and success will come like a trained falcon to its master's hand. This doesn't mean to recklessly attempt to do things that are foolish or physically unsafe. I wouldn't run a red light just because I thought

I could; I'd be gambling with mine and other's lives.

For a long time, I believed that the power of positive thinking was only a concept found in books about increasing sales and getting rich. I was completely taken by surprise when I first heard a Sufi teacher speak of thinking positively as a basic requirement to inner development. What did positive thinking have to do with learning about myself?

The Sufi's answer was that the world is what you make it. If a person only sees a world of fear, failure, and misery, it is because he or she thinks fear, failure, and misery. If one is a victim of his own self-defeating thoughts, he will also be a victim to anyone smart enough to play on his weaknesses. For instance, fear of failure may prevent one from asking for a promotion. Yet, the boss is probably looking and hoping for someone with guts enough to go for what they want because that's what it takes to get the job done.

When a person looks on a positive, hopeful world, then actions and experiences become free. The universe is infinite and human beings are mirrors that reflect that limitlessness. For the positive person, there is no end to opportunities for achievement.

Although this all sounded good in theory, I remained unconvinced. It wasn't until I experienced dramatic changes for myself that I understood the transforming power and force of positive thought.

From an early age, I had a terrifying fear of drowning. A cousin once pulled and held me below the surface of a backyard pool causing me to panic and almost drown. After this fright, I could not let my face go under water. I felt weak and helpless to push past my anxiety and I was unable to trust anyone to help me through it. My brothers and friends swam with ease, but I never lost the terror, even into my twenties.

Shortly after I met the Sufi teacher, Adnan, he came to the city where I was living to teach a weekend workshop. It was May and very hot and muggy. Undaunted by the heat, he led the group in both slow exercises and dance for hours, without stopping. I was not an athletic person, nor in very good shape, so I had trouble following all the movements.

By the middle of the second day, we had already worked intensely for several hours. We stretched, danced, bent and jumped, moving our arms and legs in hundreds of combinations. All of us were flushed from the heat. Sweat dripped down our limbs. Adnan spoke out at one point saying, *"Imagine that you are swimming now and that your sweat is the ocean all around."*

Though the rest of the group laughed at his joke, I didn't think it was funny. I couldn't swim, and now nearing the end of my patience and endurance, I felt I could no longer keep up with the bloody exercises. Yet, Adnan kept going on and on. My mind yelled *"Stop! I can't take any more."*

I almost gave up and left then, but even worse than feeling helpless, I hated that everyone would know I was running away. Adnan continued leading the exercises as if all eternity only held the movements we were doing. I made halfway efforts to keep up. A series of arm movements came, however, that were beyond my strength. The thought *"I can't do this"* rose as before.

At the end of my endurance, I was strangely, even more tired of being weak. I pushed down the thought, *"I can't!"* only to have a negative voice scream back, *"You're going to break something if you don't stop!"*

Up until this moment, I had been unaware of how much I identified with my thoughts. I was afraid to trust letting go of them, even the negative ones. Yet, because I was literally waging war against myself, I knew there was an *"I"* that existed beyond and apart from thought. It was clear, too, that this deeper self had will.

The brief touch of that will was the first stirring of an irresistible pull toward spirit. I was determined to win now. These innocent exercises had turned into a war for who called the shots, negative thoughts or positive will power.

I struggled inwardly for what seemed like hours, though it could only have been a few minutes. Then suddenly, the beast of doubt gave up and fell away, disappearing without a trace. Immediately, my arms moved as if they were as light as feathers. Both startled and exultant, I realized at once how much power negative thinking exerts over my actions and my capacity.

When the workshop finished on Sunday evening, I felt a euphoric state of serenity throughout my body and mind. I was walking out the door to leave when I heard a woman ask if there was anyone there who could give her a ride home. I said that I could take her and introduced myself as we got in my car. She lived just a few minutes away, so we chatted about the workshop while we drove to her apartment.

When we reached her place, she said there was a pool in the complex if I felt like going for a swim before I drove home. For a brief moment, I hesitated at the thought of going near the water, but then my anxiety passed. I told her I couldn't swim, but getting in the water to cool off sounded good. The night heat was stifling. Perspiration had seeped into my clothes from the day's strenuous workout, so I accepted the invitation.

My mind sensed only a quiet calmness as I waded out about midway into the pool. No fear or concern entered my thoughts, just the cool sensation of the water rippling out from my body as I moved slowly through it.

Between a thought and a command, the word entered my head, *"Swim!"* In that moment, I forgot that I could not. I pushed off with my feet and extended my arms as I recalled watching the way other people swam.

My body lifted and moved forward through the water. I swam and I floated as if I had been doing it all my life. I dared to turn over and try it on my back; it worked that way, too. I stayed in the pool for two more hours exploring my new freedom with the water. It felt like a dream, yet it was simultaneously, more real than anything else I could ever remember experiencing. A feeling of sweet contentment came over me.

I looked up at the night stars in gratitude and wonder and asked myself what had happened. In one weekend, I had just overcome twenty years of enslavement to my fear. It seemed like a miracle, but I grasped the phenomena as both primal and pragmatic. An immense amount of will power had become unbound in my body because I had refused to give into *"I can't do this."* It became clear too, how my fear had affected me not as a response to a real threat, but as a conditioned habit.

• Sometimes we feel fearful or anxious without discerning a clear reason. If a situation grips you with fear, and if you aren't in real, physical danger, try not to react. Breathe. Put your attention on your breath until the fear goes away. Sit with it, breathe into the feeling of anxiety. Follow it back inside your feelings to its origin. Look at your fear, instead of running away from it. Ask yourself, too, if you can live with the consequences of going past your fear.

• A person moving forward or making a change in life often feels that he or she may be making a mistake. Mistakes teach us; don't fear to enter that school. Anyone that says a person can learn without making mistakes is living in fantasy. Experience is the real teacher. Criticism from ourselves or from someone else only persuades us to fear trying again. If we aren't willing to risk being wrong for the sake of a dream of something better, then nothing will happen and we will always be victims of fear.

• Our fearful reactions to general economic conditions and changes in social environment may be overstimulated by the media. For instance, we have become so accustomed to the concept of working for others that when we read about the number of available jobs decreasing, we become anxious and fearful. Are we so helpless that we must always see ourselves as dependent on what others do for us?

Why don't we view the same situation as a signal for changing our life style to something possibly more rewarding, like starting our own business?

• As an exercise, make it a practice to disregard negative thoughts when they come up. Don't give them the slightest energy or foothold in your thoughts. Remember that negative thinking is simply a habit, nothing more. Thinking that you can't change is no more real than thinking that you can. You can change your thoughts by making an intention to do so and then carrying through. By refusing to surrender to negative thoughts, their power to rule you fails.

• We are spiritual beings as well as earthly creatures. Inside, there is a source of knowledge and insight about what to do in any situation, the intelligence of the heart. When we trust that the answers and even the questions come from within, fear of changing loses its hold. If fear of losing something is immobilizing you, remember that you can lose it all at any moment. Also, think of this:

"My life is on loan, like money borrowed from a bank. God is the lender, and He retains the right to call in the loan any time. Though I am responsible for taking care of it, I do not own this life; it is borrowed. Why should I fear for it's loss or anything else in this world when I must surrender it all anyway?"

If we can see that there is nothing to fear from losing the world or anything in it, we may become free of the habit of fear. We can then be open to possibilities instead of worrying about the impossible and what's not there. For many, fear to change is linked to self-defeating thought patterns. One of the most tyrannical of these patterns is the next devil, guilt.

The Third Devil:
Guilt

Guilt means feeling as if we have done something wrong, a response that often begins with family obligations. Our parents have sacrificed for us and naturally, we feel indebted to them.

Sometimes, parents or spouses will remind us of how much we owe them in order to keep us bound to their influence. Many times we become so caught up in a job, family, or marriage obligation, we can no longer recognize what's right for us. It may be necessary to first learn about our own needs in order to truly benefit or contribute to a relationship.

When my mother urged me to help my father in his business, I felt an obligation to do so. Later, when I had to make a decision to either leave or commit myself totally to the business, I was tortured by my feelings of guilt and duty. If I had stayed, it would have meant giving up what I needed for myself in order to pay back the debt I felt I owed my parents.

I also became fearful of what my parents would think of my choice. In the end, it was not an easy decision to make. I managed to disregard my apprehension for the sake of a small voice within that said *"Trust."*

This is not meant as a suggestion for anyone to quit his job. My decision came only after several weeks of daily turmoil, finally knowing with certainty that what I felt was not illusion, but the best and only course to take. I chose to risk the loss of my family's good will in order to follow my own dream. Ironically, if I had stayed because of guilt or obligation and abandoned my needs, the world I would have tried to hold on to would have been lost to me anyway.

Guilt is a poor reason for doing or not doing something. We always justify our suffering for the sake of others with a false sense of nobility, yet no one really benefits. I'm not advocating heartlessness, but if you don't know how to take care of your own needs, when you try to give to others, you are giving from a bankrupt account.

When we act out of obligation, we don't act freely. This means we don't contribute anything of value to a situation. Instead, we may feel hatred and resentment under the whip of guilt. These dark feelings can fester over time, causing us to eventually lash out from suppressed feelings in hurtful ways. We also tend to become bitter, yet righteous in justifying our sacrifice. Meanwhile, the devil of guilt continues to steal our own chance for happiness.

Guilt can also be the fear of causing someone else's unhappiness. When I first got married, I left a small, struggling business in a remote mountain area to move to where my wife lived in New York City. She had made her career there and had supported herself by teaching for many years.

I would have felt guilt in asking her to give that up in order to move where I was for the sake of my venture, now something I seemed to value less than the marriage. I let go of my business to learn other skills that would allow me to survive in the faster paced, New York environment.

It was hard to go from having complete freedom over my time to working for others again. Because I needed a job right away, I took a short training course to become a word processor through temporary help agencies. The jobs I was sent to were routine and dull, giving no feeling of satisfaction other than a steady paycheck. At least, we could be together without concerns for money.

After several months, my health began to deteriorate because of something I later learned was called "office allergy syndrome." This is a debilitating allergic reaction to the combined effects of office pollution like noise from equipment, radiation from computer monitors, formaldehyde in carpets and furnishings, recirculated air in large office buildings, and more unhealthy elements.

I began getting headaches whenever I went to work, as well as a sore throat and sinus irritation. Eventually, I could barely face going in. I'm convinced that my condition was at least partly due to forcing myself to work at a job I didn't want or enjoy.

Even though I knew it was a risk to the marriage, I felt I had to return to my previous business in the country and revive it. Surprisingly, my wife agreed and decided to try teaching free-lance in small towns, near where I had lived before moving to New York.

It wasn't long though, before she experienced unhappiness trying to teach something to people in a rural area who had little appreciation for what she had been doing so well with in New York. We finally agreed not to compromise our individual needs for each other's, which in this case, meant living in separate places. As soon as I stopped being concerned for her welfare, my own business became more successful. She equally found better success by focusing on her career needs.

In situations where one must care for a child or relative, choices become harder. Ultimately though, we are not responsible for another's happiness. The unhappy person almost always suffers from self-inflicted pain.

This unhappy individual may really need a kick in the pants to go on. More importantly, we aren't responsible for their getting better. To think otherwise is an indication that the devil of guilt has found a place in our thinking. It is also a sign of profound vanity. Do we really believe we can make other people feel happy if they don't want to do so themselves?

When we are true to ourselves, we are filling our own needs. We become full from the inside, overflowing with good will and positive intentions. In this state, we give of our time to others, because we freely choose to and because we sometimes cannot help giving.

As an exercise, do things for yourself first, once in awhile. See what happens. Take time for your projects. Go to the movie you want to see, even if it means going alone. Listen to your needs, instead of everyone else's.

If you feel guilt in relationships, either business or personal, you may need to question whether that relationship should survive. It may be holding you back. Ask yourself:

• What's the worst that will happen if I leave my job or this relationship?

• Am I putting efforts into a situation because I am full and capable of giving freely or am I giving with secret resentment?

• Am I doing what I really want in life, or do obligations and expectations fill my thoughts and direct my actions?

When we refuse to allow guilt and other devils to keep us in a holding pattern, we may be nearer to discovering our own happiness. As we move closer to knowing what we really want, however, there is another devil waiting to seduce us. Its name is vanity.

The Fourth Devil: Vanity

Vanity means pride or self-worship, which is different from self-love. In the effervescence of gaining achievement, it is easy to become enamored with oneself. You are happy having found what you want. It's so wonderful that everyone else must surely see its value, acclaim your efforts, and of course, shower you with money for doing it. Others may not all see it the same way, yet.

This is a point where you can make use of doing what you love to do to become happier and more prosperous. The trick is to not be swept off your feet by vanity, but to look for ways in which your project can be turned into a product or service with a practical application in the world. You may indeed have come up with a fantastic idea. Now is the time to see if anyone else wants or needs it. Any business which offers a product cannot survive out of vanity but must identify and fill their customers' need(s).

After leaving my family's business, I went through a series of meaningless, but expedient jobs, hoping that I would some day find a work I could love. I eventually found myself living in a mountainous area of New Mexico, learning to weave. At the same time, I began writing, though I found it frustrating and somehow intangible. By comparison, weaving seemed to satisfy a need to create something beautiful with my hands. Working with colors and rich textures opened my eyes to a new world. When customers bought my pieces, I felt a sense of accomplishment. It was a renewing experience without the claustrophobia, tedium, or politics of working for a big company.

I believed that my business background would help give me a marketing advantage over other weavers. Drawing on past experiences in retail, I began selling my work at shows and through galleries. Vanity made me imagine that my previous successes would protect me and that I would be successful because I once was. Unfortunately, I overlooked the need for homework to learn more about my trade or to keep up with current trends in the marketplace. After an initial three years of steady growth, my sales suddenly dropped to frighteningly low levels.

Unsure of how to improve the situation, I considered writing as an alternate income. Continued resistance from writer's block, however, caused doubts about whether I could succeed. I asked myself, too, if my desire to write was genuine or just vanity. Maybe I was only getting caught up with the idea of becoming an author. I did not question whether I had anything worth writing about.

Meanwhile, my weaving business was rapidly dissolving and I wondered if I would now have to start looking for a regular job. Then one day, I happened to see a copy of a *Writer's Digest* which featured an article listing the top hundred magazines for beginning authors to write for. It occurred to me that if I knew exactly who I was writing for, perhaps I could complete and sell stories to magazines. Also, I could not help feeling a tingle of vanity at the expectation of being published.

The question became *"What will I write about?"* Painful experiences especially stood out in my memory, as I felt a returning pang of regret over my failing weaving business. Certainly, I could write about the misfortune of losing a life-style I had come to cherish. I wondered, however, if I, as a reader, would care about someone else's hard luck experiences? Probably not, unless the story provided a way to resolve the problem(s) that plagued me, too.

Thinking about my weaving business, it occurred to me that other fiber artists must go through frustrations similar to mine when trying to sell their work. Where did they turn for help? Despite considerable searching, I found no reference books that answered these problems. Suddenly, I realized I was in an excellent position to help others by relating my own experiences.

At that point, a new enthusiasm took over and I reached for pen and paper. The first day, I wrote twenty-five pages; the second day, thirty-eight pages. Words flooded out. Not only had writer's block disappeared, but the process was purging the lingering pain of my business failure from my psyche. By the end of a week, I had produced over a hundred pages. Vain notions of becoming a published author had transformed into a burning desire to find the most practical answers to what others needed.

Searching bookstores and the library, I read all I could find about craft businesses. I gathered notes on the different topics and threw them into file folders. It soon became clear where I had gone wrong or might have tried a different tactic. All of this research uncovered more sales opportunities than I had ever dreamed existed.

By the time I added this new information to what I already knew from experience, I felt like an expert. I could have abandoned the writing project then and easily revitalized my business, but it felt important to first finish what I had begun. The result was a book of marketing solutions for weavers, fiber artists, and other craftspeople wanting to be in business. The book received excellent reviews and went on to sell out of two printings.

However, the taste of my initial success left me open to more subtle attacks of vanity. After my book was published, a story in itself, a distributor found it very popular with his customers and began ordering boxes of books at a time. He often congratulated me, saying how well the book was selling. Meanwhile, he was getting later and later with his payments.

At first, I ignored the problem, because he gave the book a place on the front of his catalog and displayed it at trade shows. Soon though, he owed me over $1,200 for books I had shipped on credit. When I finally realized that he was flattering me to forestall payments, I had to think of a way to get paid without losing the opportunity he provided for selling more books.

I was usually reluctant to discuss my business undertakings with friends who were not in my business. In my pride, I did not believe that someone without such experiences could grasp the situation. Ironically, it was the impulse to tell a musician friend about the distributor problem that gave me the insight needed to turn the conditions around to my favor. When I explained the circumstances, my friend, who had a clearer perspective from not being involved, reminded me that despite the collection problem, I still held the advantage. The distributor needed more books and I was the only source.

Too concerned about getting paid, I had over-looked the obvious answer.

I called the distributor the next day and explained that the book would soon be unavailable because so many overdue payments made it impossible for me to afford the cost of another printing. Fearing he might lose a highly profitable item, he offered to finance the next printing as well as pay all the overdue bills.

In all of the above incidences, I found vanity nearly ruining my success. I almost missed helpful advice from a friend because I felt I was above it. Distracted by flattery, I put off collecting money that was owed me. If I hadn't turned my vanity of being an author into providing a service to others, I might never have become published.

Feeling good about yourself is healthy. When self-love turns to self-worship, it's easy to get illusions of grandeur. As a productive counter, it is a good practice to look at your creative ideas or projects for ways in which they help others. Any small business owner will tell you that finding and filling a particular need is the key to success.

Take an activity you enjoy doing and treat it as if it were the subject of a book. Remember that you will be writing this as if others will benefit. Answering the following questions will create an outline which is really a simplified business plan that will help organize your ideas toward creating income from what you love to do:

- Clearly, what are the activities which I feel good about doing?
- Does it result in a product others will buy?
- Exactly who needs my product or service?
- How many ways are there of reaching buyers?
- What are my priorities: do I want ease of activity or more sales?
- Do I imagine that previous success exempts me from doing the homework needed to make this project work?

When what you do or create will positively help others, it can become a practical way to gain satisfaction and affluence. If the intention behind your efforts is to provide real service, the public will reward you. If, however, you just want to get rich quickly, you may be dancing with the devil of impatience.

The Fifth Devil:
Impatience

Impatience is rushing to complete an activity before its natural time. Often, we cannot tell that we're rushing a project until it's too late. A vicious devil is chasing us, but we seem unable to stop and ask, *"Why am I in a hurry?"* In trying to speed things up, we perceive situations as crises which need to be solved immediately. Projects done in haste only increase the likelihood that we will make mistakes which will cause us to have to start over again.

Impatience creates stress and stress creates more impatience. An exhausting cycle, both emotionally and physically, results in the feeling that we are surrounded by chaos and confusion. Some of the signs of impatience to obstacles or delays are obsession, tension, anxiety, nervousness, short temper, and confusion. If any of these negative feelings are present, slowing down and gaining distance from the situation will provide the advantage of a detached viewpoint.

The relaxed, unhurried person has control of his life. The calm person is more likely to look on difficulties as challenges and see opportunities where the harried person only perceives setbacks. The Sufis, as well as mental health researchers, have found that creative insights are more likely to occur in states of calm. The higher functions of the brain such as holistic perception and intuition tend to be inoperative under stress. The more relaxing activities we do, like the ones at the end of this chapter, the more intuitive and creative we become. We become more sensitive to the natural intelligence in our hearts. Our attention is gathered and ready for anything. We see our way clearly. We use time more fully instead of feeling chased by it.

When I was putting together the material for my book for fiber artists, I had no idea how, or even if, I could get it published. Without previous writing credits, I had minuscule hope of getting noticed by book editors. Also, the number of potential readers needing a book about the marketing of fiber art was probably too small for a large publisher to see any profit margin.

Alternately, it occurred to me that I could publish the book myself. To do this, of course, I would need a number of new skills I did not have. I found the idea intriguing, though and so I began learning what it meant to self-publish.

Excited about becoming an author in print, I rushed to borrow several hundred dollars to purchase equipment, books, and supplies based on the recommendations of the publishing guides. If I had been patient and done more homework, I could have saved a lot of money and time. Most of these initial purchases contributed little to the book's publication or sales.

Self-publishing required that I learn how to write clearly as well as to edit, typeset, print, advertise, and sell the book. When I began to see that mastering these new skills wouldn't happen in a few days or even weeks, I became impatient. I began to fear that someone else might come up with a similar book before I could complete mine.

Also, despite my original intention to write something of use to others, my ego still hungered for imagined fame and fortune. I was dancing to the tunes of the devils of vanity and impatience. Meanwhile, financial considerations pressed me as well. By this time, I was just getting by on a tiny income from straggling sales of my woven pieces and some part-time work.

In my initial calculations, I expected the writing and publishing process to take about six months and $4,000 to $5,000 in start-up money. It was now almost a year later, the book was still unfinished, and actual costs were reaching $10,000, which I had managed to borrow.

Amidst these pressures to finish the book and begin marketing it, I suddenly faced the prospect of setting the entire project aside. My teacher, Adnan, called and suggested I join him in Los Angeles where he would be teaching workshops for a few weeks. The invitation seemed odd to me, because after several years of working with him, he rarely suggested anymore that I travel to meet him.

My first thought was *"No,"* now was not the time to go. I couldn't possibly afford to take time off when so many different elements of the project required action. I felt that if I didn't complete the book soon, I would have to give up my dream and look for a steady job. I didn't want that. The book, like a needy child, was crying for immediate attention.

Almost convinced of my reasons not to go to L.A., I then remembered how following Adnan's advice to quit my family business had saved me from making a major financial mistake. Adnan seemed to offer his counsel at times when I least expected or wanted to hear it. In these situations, I was often in danger of making decisions based on logic or impulse alone, without accessing that intuitive guidance that comes from listening to what's going on inside. Through Adnan's timely interventions, he led me first to have faith in his intuition and later, in my own. Trusting this would be the case again this time, I decided to put aside the book and join him in Los Angeles.

I was completely unaware how bound up I had become until I started putting the miles between the project and myself. Time slowed as

I drove and relaxed, and became absorbed by the natural purity of the desert landscape. When I reached the pollution and traffic of Los Angeles, I found the change of scenery less compelling.

Despite the city's pace, Adnan's workshop soon dissolved any lingering sense of my previous obsession. Once I connected with the revitalizing spirit of the Sufi work, I felt at ease and relaxed. Thoughts about my book occasionally came up, but the internal pressure was gone. I accepted the fact that I would simply deal with it when I returned home. Detached from my impatience, even the L.A. traffic seemed remote. Where were all these cars going in such a hurry, I wondered? The cars on the freeway seemed the perfect metaphor of my thoughts when I'm in a hurry. They race compulsively on a selected course, heedless of the world around them. I also noted that like on the freeway, I could take an exit ramp at any time if I needed to relax awhile.

By the time I returned home a couple of weeks later, I felt confident that I could easily pick up the book again from where I had left it. When I examined the manuscript, though, I couldn't believe what I was staring at. Everything was wrong; scores of grammatical errors I had previously overlooked seemed to jump off the pages. Worse yet, the whole organization of the book was snarled. I had been in such a rush that I had failed to see what a mess I was creating.

Diligently and patiently, I began reworking the manuscript. My only concern now was to do the job right. Debts and deadlines could wait. Ironically, my starting over again with this new intention of creating a perfect work, rather than getting it done as soon as possible, actually sped the editing process.

An image of the book as a complete whole appeared in my mind and the proper organization took shape. This revision turned into a major rewrite, but a better book emerged, one that was both cohesive and useful.

Soon it was time to submit the completed manuscript for review. My patience was rewarded when a major crafts publication, *The Crafts Report* said, among other good things, that the book *"should be considered the blueprint for success in the crafts industry."* This review sparked orders from around the country. More publications soon mentioned the book as well. Distributors began ordering one hundred copies at a time because they were getting so many calls. Within seven months of the first printing, 1,000 copies had sold and another 1,000 needed to be printed. The second printing sold out even sooner.

If I had given in to the devil of impatience, I would have sent out a messy, disorganized text, full of so many errors no reviewer would have considered it. Stepping back and gaining distance had opened my eyes to the necessity of creating the best possible work which subsequently led to excellent reviews and sales.

Remember that acting impatiently may result in having to do something all over again. It can also lead you away from doing the necessary homework to ensure your business survives. When starting a new business, it almost always takes more time than you can imagine.

Relaxation is the solution to impatience. Sometimes this may mean walking (or driving) away from the situation for awhile, even though this is often the most difficult thing to do when under the whip of haste. However, there are several excellent ways of training the mind to relax, get in the moment, and encourage creativity:

- Do things that put you in a peaceful, relaxed state of mind, for example: walking, exercise, baking cookies, working in the yard or garden.
- Write about the things that happen to you in a daily journal.
- Spend several hours in nature once or twice a week. A walk through the woods communicates the suggestion of the clean and gentle spirit of nature — trees don't hurry. Insights can arise freely in a calm, unhurried mind.
- Dance, make music, create art; these are all effective ways to reverse impatience. They are pure fun, good for relaxing the body, and you don't have to be in a hurry to make something happen.
- Meditate or sit quietly doing nothing for at least ten minutes, twice a day. This is a good time to do the breathing exercise on page 77.
- Learn a craft. The process will not only develop patience, it soothes tension and stress. Occupational therapists teach crafts to sufferers

of stress because it calms and focuses the mind and body.

All of the devils talked about until now — false success, fear, guilt, vanity, and impatience — are habits or learned behavior patterns. They can be unlearned and replaced by positive patterns. If we don't confront them, they will imprison us in slave mentality. To be a slave to the devil of habit is to invite a thousand other masters to rule our decisions.

The Sixth Devil: Habit

Anything done mechanically and without awareness is a habit. Habits can be physical, mental, emotional, or any combination of these. Some examples include: getting up at the same time every morning, having the same foods for breakfast, driving the same way to work, and reading the newspaper every evening.

Although some routines may seem harmless, the danger in any habit is its tendency to lull us to sleep. We miss the opportunity to act in the moment, because we engage in old patterns. In order to hear the intelligence of the heart, be on the alert for any habitual thinking or behavior that restricts your creative flow. You can counter the devil of habit by learning to awaken and utilize your creativity through many of the exercises mentioned in this book.

The tendency to repeat an action originates early. It is the infant's way of seeking control over its world by playing back or imitating actions that parents show. As the child grows, rewards reinforce the patterns of behavior and begin to shape the basis of the personality or the ego.

Often in our early training, the intuitive, intelligence of the heart is forgotten, though this does not mean it isn't there. Almost everyone experiences occasional insights and mental breakthroughs that transcend the boundaries of common logic.

Sufi teachers, like Adnan, have noted that intuitive perception is sometimes a natural by-product of their training, though it is seen as a stage in the process of development, not an end in itself.

Relaxing quietly and doing enjoyable activities helps overcome the compulsion of habits and stimulate the flow of innovative answers to difficulties.

Of course, some habits like eating right and exercising regularly keep us fit and healthy. As you get closer to learning and doing what you really want in life, you may find self-defeating habits falling away. On the other hand, bad habits may have become so conditioned that you need to confront them in order to free yourself from their effects.

In my early twenties, I had the habit of drinking two bottles of cola almost everyday. One day, the notion occurred to me that I might be addicted. Disliking such external control, I decided to stop the next day. I was amazed to find myself trembling by early afternoon and finally reaching for the soda.

What concerned me more than anything else was the awareness that I was the captive of a material substance. If a small amount of carbonated liquid held that much sway over my will, what larger influences were also affecting my decisions? With considerable effort, I managed to stop the habit for two months. By then, I had lost the desire for the cola again and realized through this that habits can be broken.

Later, when I first began to run my own business, I discovered that money came in at unpredictable intervals. Surprisingly, even several months after I started, the thought would recur that I would be better off if I left my business to look for work with a large company. I was still conditioned to expect a weekly paycheck, a pattern developed from the years of working for others. When I didn't give into these internal tapes and found I was still surviving, these urges to get a "real" job eventually faded away. From this experience, I realized that many choices we make may come from conditioned patterns of response.

Since I had not surrendered to my conditioning, the energy and effort I would have put into some other company's profits went instead, into the growth and success of my own enterprise. Of course, being single at the time, I had no family to support and there were no other considerations of responsibility.

We have learned to think and react in patterns because our education focuses on memorization and calculation. This discipline strengthens reliance on memory and mental habits, yet ignores the need for being ready for the unexpected. Because of our early training with facts, we also tend to assign authority to much of what we read. Realistically though, is it wise to believe something just because its printed on paper? This tendency may be a cultural mechanism inherited from the days when writing belonged to priests in the old religions. People once believed that written words were magical and only priests were wise enough to use their power. Yet, intelligence is more than believing words or accumulating facts. It is better measured by how we handle the unexpected, as almost every new business owner discovers when survival often depends on finding novel solutions.

After winning the battle against my programmed urges to find a real job, I discovered a wellspring of creativity flowing into my work. I also began to review everyday practical decisions in the light of my intuition. It seemed that if one could discern and access the intuitive perception, success would come in a natural, organic way.

When I acted on this trust, I often experienced less stress when encountering unexpected situations like when dealing with distributors and other publishers who had more experience than I.

Our habits of response are measurable and send a clear signal to others who are always ready to take advantage of our vulnerability. They have learned how specific words can make us feel excited, fearful, aroused, or guilty. If we allow them to, they will tell us what to think, what to buy, what to eat, and even what to become. Our habits will support them. Sometimes these others will use our habits to take even more from us, like everything they can.

A friendly editor for a large publisher had agreed to revise and reprint my first book. She sent an initial contract, assuring me that it was a standard agreement which I just needed to sign and return. From her smooth manner, I assumed that this was a mere formality and nothing to be concerned about. Not having a lawyer, I almost did this for the sake of expediting the publication process. Something warned me, however, to look over the papers more closely.

With the help of a book on negotiating contracts, I examined the agreement, paragraph by paragraph. I found disturbing financial obligations on my part couched in legalese which the editor never brought up in our previous friendly talks. If I had signed the paper as it was, I would have committed to pay out additional expenses almost equal to the publisher's advance.

This incident and another that followed made me realize that this woman intended to get whatever she could from me in the way of money and publishing rights. It seemed she was pulling from a bag of old tricks she had used successfully with other authors whose habitual responses had been predictably reliable. Because this business is so competitive, many authors may be so fearful of not getting published, they eagerly sign away all their rights. Fortunately, I saw what she was doing and I was able to pull out of the arrangement before she stole legal and financial control of my book.

Other emotional reactions can be habits, too, stimulated when we receive a particular cue. For instance, we may always cry at a sad movie, get angry whenever our lover looks at someone else, or become predictably excited when there's a sale on at our favorite store. Emotions play a large role in self-defeating patterns like smoking and overeating. For instance, when the boss is over critical about his work, an employee may find himself compulsively eating candy bars in an attempt to restore his self esteem. A solution is to watch and learn to recognize the difference between what happens when we act from habit and what happens when we act from clear choice.

Adnan, in his work with people of different backgrounds, specializes in eliminating all kinds of self-defeating habits like smoking and alcohol abuse, not because these things are "bad" but because habits enslave the person. When a person gets in touch with the positive forces within themselves, they no longer need or desire superficial habits.

As an exercise, breaking daily routines can help bring one more into the present. I've noticed that in almost all instances where I faced a new situation or difficulty, habitual patterns of problem solving failed to meet the challenge. Being flexible and ready for the unknown always gave me a better chance of success.

• Make a point of examining your reactions in different situations. Are you acting out old patterns automatically? Might these patterns be keeping you from seeing alternate possibilities or opportunities?

• Try breaking routines to see what happens. Instead of turning on the television, exercise or work on a creative project. Replace that next cigarette or candy bar with a twenty minute walk. Exercise often eliminates these artificial needs.

• Often habits are indicative of avoidance behavior. Are you trying to compensate for fear of failure, guilt, or obligation? Do things for yourself that feed your own needs for self-esteem. Then, you'll feel like embracing life instead of avoiding it.

When we are under their control, habitual thoughts or actions distract us from reality and cut us off from the voice of our intelligence of the heart. Is there more to life that we may be missing? The answer to that question lies beyond our plans for the future or our reliance on old solutions. The most powerful tool for accessing creative insight is right in front of us. It is the awareness of the here and now. This ever flowing source of strength and renewal is often forgotten though, because of one last nefarious devil, seeing time as a clock.

The Seventh Devil:
The Clock

Perhaps the most insidious and illusory devil of all is time when we perceive it as the clock. Though useful in a scheduled world for meeting deadlines, the clock can easily enslave us to the illusion of its sovereignty. When this occurs, we lose track of the only true asset we have in this life, the moment in our hands. *Here and now* is the source and life spring of creativity. It is the doorway to the answers to our problems.

As children, we experienced time as open-ended and full of wonder. We lived our creativity in play, barely touched by the demands of the clock. Life flowed and time was full. After many of us reached the age of responsibility, the experience of being present in the moment was lost to a multitude of schedules and agendas.

The conception of time as a clock, an outside object separate from our inner experience, is a trained perception just like any other habit. The artificial rhythm of the clock replaces our own natural rhythm, yet everything in nature has its proper time and season. Are humans apart from nature that they don't heed this rhythm? The devil of the clock pushes the organic, natural time of any project, but worse, it pushes you toward an artificial reality.

This is not to say that we should never plan. A business owner, for instance, could not survive without shaping out a course. However, the planning process can turn on you like a mad dog, consuming your life with its rabid demands.

Remember that planning is illusory projection, based on what might be, not what is. Plans must be flexible and ready for anything that comes in the moment. The world never stays the same. Survival and success have always come naturally to those who are instantly ready to adapt in nature or in business.

Instead of being focused and awake to what's in front of us, many of our thoughts are worries about what has happened in the past and what will happen next.

By allowing more time for ourselves, we can break the clock routine and regain the real time, that is the natural, inherent aliveness that makes one's moments happy and beautiful.

A wonderful description of this state appears in the book of Sufi stories, *When Life is Lovable and Love is Livable* by Adnan Sarhan.

"The glow, the spark and the fire of life at its best exists in the present. And the present exists in the moment where life is pure, beautiful, delightful and contented. And the time and space become like heaven, and the heaven comes to them and fills them with tranquility, intelligence of the heart and the extract of life unknown to the rational, intellectual mind. And the heart, the space and the time fly in each others arms like drops of water when they mix and become all water — no separation, no division and no conflict is left."

Many of us see glimpses of the real time in the moment of creative flow, when we are surprised, when we first visit a new place, when we eat a new food, and sometimes not until we face near death like when having a heart attack. The breathing exercise below and the relaxing exercises beginning on page 60 will help restore that remembrance of what it means to be *here and now.* I say restore, because the moment is the reality we have only misplaced. Is there any good reason why daily life must exclude this experience of aliveness and wakefulness? If we look for it, work can be play and play can lead to enjoyable success through creativity.

How often have you felt that there is no time in your schedule to do what you really want? How many times have you said, *"I'll do it later, when I have more time."* We put off our desires, because in our secret vanity, we believe that we will live forever. Death happens to the other guy, not us. We ignore our mortality, but when death is invisible to us, so is life. The Sufis have a saying, *"Opportunity is precious and time is a sword."* The power to achieve whatever you want from life is in your hands right now. It may not be there tomorrow.

The Sufis also use the breath to bring one to the moment in practices which can develop higher states of perception. Interestingly, science has determined that in humans, 40% of the oxygen taken in is used by the brain. It seems that nature may have designed a natural link between our breathing and our intelligence. For the most part, though, we never think about our breath, yet our life totally depends upon this fragile, immutable process. It sustains our existence, moment by moment. We may ignore breath, but it never ignores us, until the end when it's finished forever.

Once at a workshop, my teacher, Adnan, led a group of us in chanting a word, *Shafi,* (Shaa fee) one of the names or attributes of God in Arabic. *Shafi* has meanings on many levels; one is to heal and another is to change anything negative to positive.

Sitting cross legged on the floor, we were to inhale *Sha* and exhale *fi* moving the head slowly and alternately toward each knee, inhaling *Sha* up again and exhaling *fi* down to the other knee in continuation. The instruction was to keep the mind concentrated on the sound, the breath, and the movement.

Though I had practiced chanting before, this time my mind felt unusually focused. After a few minutes of following the sound, my concentration deepened and the awareness of my breath, the feeling of movement, and the sound of *Shafi* suddenly fused together.

As the three elements merged, I felt swept into an overwhelming awareness of a single, perpetual moment of time. This moment seemed to tremble from the fullness of limitless creativity and incredible strength of will. No doubt or confusion remained in my insufficient mind, only awe and humility at the immensity of the creative force of the universe. Power to act and to change was within my reach, but required no reaching; it was there inside — it is always there in all of us if we want it. I knew then, that if one could become aware of this power inside the present moment, nothing in the world would keep one from succeeding except oneself.

As an exercise, find a place to be alone, preferably in nature. Close your eyes. Breathe deeply and slowly. Follow your inhaling and exhaling with complete attention.

Concentration may not come easily, the habit of thinking will not want to give up control. Distractions may try to seduce you saying you are wasting time, there are places to go, fancy foods to eat, and more important things to worry about. It doesn't matter what the thoughts say, keep bringing the awareness back to the breath. Stay with this exercise for at least ten to fifteen minutes.

Then, look around the nature that surrounds you. See and hear the world of the moment you are in. You may begin to notice how dependent you are on breath, that, in fact, you are not breathing at all, you are being breathed. Your life is in the hands of a greater force and each breath is a gift.

When you return to your work, or spouse, or any other concerns, remember the gift of life. Carry it with you into the next moment. Let the purity of the present replace confusion with awareness and clarity.

If we follow our heart's desire, the devil of false success cannot lure us into an unfulfilling future built on others' expectations. Unreasonable fears from the past will have no hold on us. Vanity and impatience will not steal our success from under us. We will replace self-defeating habits with awareness of new possibilities.

In the experience of the moment, the intelligence of the heart will awaken and transcend the powers of all the seven devils to become a magic genie that brings you wisdom, joy, and happiness. Now, there are no devils. Everywhere you turn, there is wonder, delight, and opportunities. Time is your friend and will guide you to discover your own secret dream and how to realize it.

About the author . . .

James Dillehay weaves and writes in the mountains of central New Mexico. In addition to three books, he is also consulting editor for *Tantra Magazine* and reviewer for *Small Press Magazine.* His essays on Sufi experience have appeared in publications by the Sufi Foundation.

About Adnan Sarhan . . .

Sufi Master Adnan Sarhan is director of the Sufi Foundation of America. Internationally known for the Shattari (Rapid) Method, his work develops higher intelligence and awareness through a wide range of timeless techniques. Exercises, meditation, drumming, movement, dancing and whirling are used to heighten concentration and produce bodily changes, including slower heart rates, lower blood pressure, and shifts in perception opposite to those caused by stress.

Over the years, Adnan has conducted workshops at prestigious institutions throughout the U.S. and many other countries including: the United Nations in New York, The World Congress of Psychology in Switzerland, The Earth Summit in Brazil and conferences of Humanistic Psychology. Each summer he directs an intensive two-month seminar at the Sufi Foundation Retreat Center in the Manzano Mountains of New Mexico. For further information about that program, contact: Sufi Foundation, P.O. Box 170, Torreon, NM 87061.

From: *The Enchanted Oasis of the Ringed Dove* by Adnan Sarhan

"You are only living when you are graced and blessed in the moment, by the moment. The moment is the fountain of serenity. The moment says, "I am a messenger to you, a messenger of eternity. I bring you a message of eternal joy. I am joy and tranquility. I am peace and delight. I am faith and trust. I am truth and reality. I am in the moment because I am the moment. I am honor, respect and dignity. I am simple, tolerant and generous.

"I am the time and the time is me. I am the profound depth of intelligence and intelligence is me. I am the beautiful spring of essence and essence is me. I am the perfume of life and the fragrance of a smile. I am the living spark and spirit that shines in the eyes. I am the sweet taste of heaven and I am heaven in your heart. I am charm, beauty, delight, happiness, tranquility, serenity and the pleasure of life and I am in the present all the time. With you, I am the moment that never fades, that never goes away."

by Adnan Sarhan

The Enchanted Oasis of the Ringed Dove, 5" X 8", 96 pp, softcover, ISBN: 1-884328-01-6, $7.95, printed on recycled papers from Sufi Foundation of America, P.O. Box 170, Torreon, NM 87061